BURNING ORACLE

ALSO BY SANDRA SIMONDS

POETRY

Triptychs
Atopia
Orlando
Further Problems with Pleasure
Steal It Back
The Sonnets
Mother Was a Tragic Girl
Warsaw Bikini
Combustible Mood (chapbook)

FICTION

Assia

WESLEYAN POETRY

BURNING ORACLE

Sandra Simonds

*

Wesleyan University Press

Middletown, Connecticut

Wesleyan University Press
Middletown CT 06459
www.weslpress.org

Manufactured in the United States of America
Designed and typeset in Parkinson Electra
by Eric M. Brooks

Library of Congress Cataloging-in-Publication Data
available at https://catalog.loc.gov/
paper ISBN 978-0-8195-0216-2
ebook ISBN 978-0-8195-0217-9

5 4 3 2 1

. . . throw yourself

out of yourself

* PAUL CELAN

CONTENTS

BURNING ORACLE

ON REYNARD

DO: His pelt is orange, unless he lives in the Arctic; because our story is set in Paris, his pelt is orange.

RE: In the Arctic, his coat changes from white in the winter to blue in the summer to blend with the sky.

MI: In medieval tales, he fakes his own death and when the animals (wolf, rooster, lion, dog) gather to mourn him at the funeral, he pops out of his casket, terrifying them.

FA: Cardinals represent the morning; Reynard is a symbol of evening.

SOL: His laughter as he jumps from the grave and chases the animals through the cemetery can be heard throughout Paris.

LA: Legend has it that when Reynard's pelt turns blue, he can pass himself off as a peacock.

TI: Reynard builds his house of ice; the hare builds her house with hay.

DO: When spring comes and Reynard's house melts, he pursues the hare, steals her home, and reads "Death Fugue" by Paul Celan on his sofa.

TI: If he understood love, he would be in love with Cassandra.

LA: Who understands love? Not a fox.

SOL: In ancient Egypt, the fox plays the lute; in France, he is known as "le fuckboy."

FA: *Then Samson went and caught three hundred foxes; and he took torches, turned the foxes tail to tail, and put a torch between each pair of tails.*

MI: Who understands the fox? Not prophecy.

RE: Aristophanes notes Reynard's predilection for eating grapes.

DO: Samson watches the waves of fire roar through the fields, olive trees, vineyards; out of the corner of his eye, he catches Rey dart away.

1)

Rey's blood-
red brush swishing
the centuries,
tail held high
over Paris, above
consciousness
triangular teeth
crunching
antique glass
grapes, a bunch
of tricks raised
from the dead
of flesh,
metro line
the aorta
that hurls us
through decades,
he glides,
I glide, one
millimeter above
the Seine, astral
paws projecting behind
his fables, my
tales, to shred
time with claws,
fingernails,
etch two
trails of river
water: we came
to this land
by violence,

propelled
into city, country,
wars to locate
a center inside
our autumn-
colored all-fours,
nonhuman form,
one path to the future,
the other, unknown.

*

Rey called.
I told him
not to; he kept
calling. He said he
didn't know
why I turned
him on.
Me neither?
I hid in a large
field of aster.
It was May,
a time
of purples. May,
the optimal.
I answered that
I live a bad life,
and that I'm mad.
Shoot me
a picture
of your lament.
How near
the hue of kinesis,
these spring

waters, I answered.
He wrapped
himself tightly
in my prepositions,
sent a verb or two
between my thighs.
Oh, it was the good
kind of love,
unencumbered by love.
In the morning,
I noticed he'd left
behind his blood-
red gloves.
May, the sick days,
the many-
rayed clouds.

*

The clouds
have become
broomsticks
and upside-
down seahorses.
Francisco tells
the world he's
mad, and at age
forty-six, he's
gone deaf. No
one listens, so
he locks
himself up in
the Magic
View Motel,
begins painting

her visions —
dancing bears, Moose
Crossing signs —
rattles the vertical
chain lines
of his cage.
How is he able
to hear Cassandra
dreaming?
Paints the walls —
two witches
spinning wool,
a paper cap
worn by victims
of the Inquisition.
Laura doesn't visit.
Back again in the semi-
darkness. He says
he's trapped
by her images
that flow
on the other
side. Of what?
Of barriers.

*

You're late.
I'm never late.
She checks her phone —
flow of ads —
Rock Point
School Vermont.
Learn more. Baby
aardvark riding

on mother's
back, best way to
slow graying –
Rey's an hour
and a half late.
Busy doing
some work,
he says, eyes
glued to phone.
Argument
in the car
on the way
to the party.
Rey swerves
off the road.
She holds a glass
bowl of water-
melon salad
in her lap,
juice splashing on
her yellow
polka-dotted dress.
Francisco opens
the front door.
You made it!
Come in, come in!
Laura sitting
in the corner
waiting to speak
to someone.
Francisco happier
than usual, taking a new
antidepressant.
I can't make art,

but at least
I no longer
see witches
in my pancakes.
So, I hear
you're going to
Paris in October?
Yes, she's going
to research her family,
Rey says, patting
Cassandra on the head.
You know, the ones
murdered in the camps.
Rey says she's saved
enough to buy a plane
ticket to Paris patting . . .
pat pat pat.
Francisco puts his
hand on her
shoulder. *You should*

*

be very proud . . .
. . . of the things left
in childhood—trapping
fireflies in jars, the pony's
enormous teeth,
lips, the farm
in the south of France,
too much of the story, too
little—my great-
grandparents
from Turkey
won the lottery

in 1936. Shot of
my grandmother
walking in Nice,
locking arms
with her sister. Again.
Look
at it again,
again. Epi-
genetically,
you stare. One month
after the liberation.
This shot. Roar
of trains, screeching
lore, the farm thrown
into the century's mouth,
to say my grandfather
was poor. In November, unlucky.
December, poor. The century
turns him to a boy of sixteen
who wants to see *The Wizard*
of Oz, twists light
in a crystal,
turns to one
of his Catholic friends,
who passes him an identity
card, the wounded
crystal's light
is a trail, every-
thing in my family was
compared to the war.
You feel sick? You're fine,
your grandparents
lived through the war.

Does this machine
deserve the details?
My grandfather walked
to the mountains, blew
up trains, barns.
Horses. Ponies. Chickens.
Jars. Another
shot, another
mother born, ma,
mom, mama a few
months after ah
the liberation.
Every century
turns up
its wounds.

*

Everyone
turns up
in the backyard
counting down 5, 4,
3, 2 . . . . Rey kisses
Cassandra
on the lips.
Bang!
Next Year has
officially
begun.
Bang! Bang!
I'm unhappy
in this marriage,
Rey says on
the way home.

Let's take
some time apart.
(No one knows
who says this.) Bang!
The watermelon
juice has dried
into a pink blotch
on her dress.
Rey finds a hotel.
Blotch: seahorse?
Spends the night there.
Blotch: squid?
Bang!
Bang!

*

Strangely colored sky,
the air bad
—smoke billowing
into Vermont
from above Montreal:
an onyx snake
gone into a hole.
Ash rain. Massive
forest fires. What
is health, anyway,
to an artist?
I'm nothing
but green lightning,
a psychic conduit.

*

Or a consensual
hallucination *Green Living*

measured in behavioral
surplus *Life Hacks*
and footfalls forgiving
We have the right
to be forgotten
Fine machine I do like
Air Travel Fine fine
machine twitching past
the grassy comets
along the forefinger of
Offer Discounts
the Seine I bought
an old book with a Max Ernst
etching wonderful
eddies algo moon
Use Testimonials
poems calyxing
in the death garden
Keep It Personal
and wondered if this
is where you jumped
into triangles squares
Play on Nostalgia
of river water plunged
as I entered
the hypotenuse of
stone names
or auras
etched high
as pillars with my
index finger
I ran down
the names
kneeled until

there stop
touched the surname
of my family

*

Name? Cassandra.
Gloved hand tosses around books in suitcase.
Picks up one of them.
What's this?
It's a book.
Tosses it on a lavender bra.
You've come to? Visit the grave of Paul Celan.

*

Please
step back
from the concourse.
Write
a lopsided family history.
Wrap
yourself with the name ropes.
Trace
the quasi-stellar radio source of time with your forefinger.
Weigh
the metaphors on the bathroom scale.
Weave
the insignia of your bloodline with my vocal cords.
Touch
the engraved eye sockets.

*

Collection of gazes 1869
at the Musée d'Orsay short movie

Man in a top hat   collapses at the foot
of a Galatea statue   *Come to life!*

Her eyes   flutter open
She walks   toward him in a toga

His body   convulses   to gold light
Crypt of history   stone   hands

I look down   at the pink blotch
dead seahorse   stone

nightmares   the conjured
too powerful   for the conjurer

*

Second day
of the New Year.
Cassandra stays in bed,
reads a book
on Astral Projection.
Make me some crêpes!
It's Chloe.
Can't muster
enough energy.
Lou, the Pomeranian,
shits in the house.
Can't walk him.
Been raining
for two weeks.
Calls Rey.
Straight to voicemail.
Throws laptop
across the room.

Crack in the screen is
 a bolt of jade lightning,
 picks up the stereoscopic image
 on her bedside table:

Inscription: *Women Washing Clothes in the Seine.*
She tears it in half.
The Destroyer of Things
has become her personality.

*

Inside Cassandra,
 the book burned,
 her body flooded, burned.
Fires in July, floods in August,
drowned by October. A deer
 found the ashes
 in the river and laughed, ate
 them raw. The stag
 was hit by a car, and it snowed
 for the first time in Florida
 in two-hundred years.
 The people called it a strange
 white rain. It was a dream
 where I wrote my life
 story in the language
 of cirrus clouds, the sky

cleared, could not be retold
in any ordinary sense of the word *tale*.
The fox was a foil for her desires, travels,
and past. He was a bad fox, then good,
then bad again, tricked her into thinking
the world was slanted
a certain way. Beware, Cassandra,
beware the machine, for it will extract
your story from you — all things reduced
to tags and pixels: double clicks, custom audience —
then spit you out the other end.
He was right, that little Rey, in October,
November, and soon, if I'm able
to recall the details, you will
recognize my book in the deer's
maddening body of decomposing leaves.

*

You're impossible, Rey says.
Paul: *Who breaks no ground?*
Cassandra: *I couldn't*
fit inside
the poem
I made,
the poem growing
horns to replace
myth with this.
With what? A realness.
Paul: *Your poem is undermost.*
Francisco: *I didn't want to be impossible.*

I wanted to say things to you. (all of us).

ON CASSANDRA

1. Her mother was a pit viper and only spoke French at home.
2. She was left with her sister to stay in an apartment with an abusive boyfriend who did terrible things to both girls.
3. Cassandra sparkles like an eyeball, chandelier, or droplet of water.
4. Her mother had a chaos-sensing pit on both sides of her head between her eyes and nose that drew her prey into it; the girls were prey.
5. Cassandra wears a gold lion necklace she found at Goodwill and never takes it off.
6. Her hair is always on fire, and if someone tries to put it out with water, the fire grows.
7. Her prophesies are built on the Ache Ruins, and the Ache Ruins are built on her prophesies.
8. Ten minutes after she wakes, she dies; this cycle is repeated daily.
9. Her mother was a drunk and would stay in bed passed out for days while her daughters foraged the house for food.
10. One day in her teen years, on a visit to New Orleans, she met Reynard in a bar, and they spoke about their childhoods and agreed that they had more in common than most.
11. Reynard and Cassandra, both high in Missoula, Montana, get into a domestic dispute in their apartment. The police are called. Both are arrested, given community service. Reynard picks trash up off the side of the road until he finds the right moment, when the police are not paying attention to the prisoners, and runs off.
12. In middle age, overwhelmed with grading papers, she takes a trip to Paris to research her family members, most of whom were murdered in concentration camps.
13. Reynard sends a text to Cassandra while she is in Paris telling her that she has a beautiful body and he loves her poetry. He says that he thinks of her when he fucks his new girlfriend.
14. She teaches a class on Holocaust Literature in the fall, one on Confessional Poetry in the spring.

15. In the spring, when the world is most beautiful and the blue tulips burst from the mossy earth, she is more likely to text Reynard and less likely to think about her past or her family history.
16. When a well-known poet dies, she has a vision of ruined meadowland exactly ten hours before the death.
17. In the Holocaust Literature class, she passes around a peculiar stone she found at Paul Celan's grave and shares the documents of her great-uncle Jacques, who survived Auschwitz only to die later at Flossenbürg, a concentration camp deep in Bavaria.
18. She cannot stand the sound of chewing.
19. She has incredible fashion sense, especially when she dresses like a lava lamp.
20. Her favorite artist is Francisco Goya; a print of *Yard with Lunatics* hangs in her office.

11)

I roam the Luxembourg Gardens
in apotropaic lusters,
in my long, cherry
leather skirt
from the last century,
ruby eye-
lashes, hell-red nails, roam
one instance
at a time as history
circulates
the bloodstream
in strange ash
and crescents.
There's more
to the story —
that my mother
tried to kill herself
my first year of college,
that when I came back
home from rollerblading,
she was lying
by the front door,
that was the day
I understood *Real*
Estate Websites
that I had spent those years
drinking and fucking
men women
anyone old young
didn't matter to me
trying to forget

Paper Art
that I was a little
shoplifter too—starting with nail
polish and eyeliner, ending
with bras, underwear,
a pair of satin gold
pants from a shop on
Westwood Blvd., the shop owner
chased me
down the street,
yelled *thief*
but I just wanted to
Holy Ghost
it all away, let beauty
just happen, inhale the plants,
I could become exhaust—
someone without a past,
without countries,
or the bullshit of stories,
or the maternal,
because when my mother
looked at me, I reminded her
of everything she hated,
the heavy lineage
no one should have to carry,
now I understand
what that means, to
have to carry
a story from one
country to the next,
one year
to the next, this river
that rests in the little
thumping heart

of an infant, who
        would ever
          want that?   I get it.
                                        I get it.

*

No source, my Seine,
a German one instead,
sixteen and reading Hölderlin's
"Der Rhein" at the foot of a massive
statue of Goethe and Schiller.
Stupid anorexic American girl.
But not *really* American.
And not *really* French.
And not *really* Turkish.
And not *really* Syrian.
And not *really* Spanish.
And the tourists at the camp.
    Was I a tourist?
Squeal of the cassette
    tape rewinding
Pink Floyd's *The Wall.*
Ah, when you speak German,
    no one can tell
you're American. When you speak
   English, no one can tell
you're French. Too sick to go on.
                Anne of Green Gables figurines.
I'm always too sick
    to go on, that's
my charm — a gray
ruin turned maroon
turned black.

*

It is easier to go mad,
Francisco says,
than one might think.

Easy to lose things.
People too.
Perhaps too easy.
Step inside
and you may not
come back.

He listed the colors he liked:
Black.
Black.
Black.
Black.
He told himself
to stay inside the painting
of the chartreuse river,
stay inside, Reader,
and he found his arms
roping and looping
into Cassandra
holding a tray
of dead pigeons.

*

Reynard, I've seen
you with a dying pigeon
in your snout, out-
witting the backyard
pugs on YouTube

by diving
into a hole
and coming
out the other
side unscathed,
but I have also
seen you flayed
as in *Gawain*,
turned to red
pelt for display,
your innards
mixed with bread
and wine, a slurry
delivered
to the ravenous.
Won't you
tell the truth?
I've felt such affection
for you, even
going so far as
to send you
ochre nudes.
Yet I, too,
am a faltering
illusion, keep
my phone on silent
through the delirium
of days.
Foxy R.,
we're all lonely
and can only trick
ourselves into
believing otherwise
for so long.

*

Rey stops by after work.
  Sixth Week of the Year
  of the Rat
and he's still living
  at the Old Carrabelle Hotel.
A tropical abyss.
  Live oaks fall
across the city.
Chloe is washing
  quarters in the bathroom.
Which one is shinier?
  she asks, holding out
two quarters.
  (Cassandra chooses
the right hand.)
  This one?
Wrong, Mom.
  Rey pours himself
a cup of coffee.
  Z comes out of his room
looking like an animal
  emerging from a cave.
Dad, he says
  lowering his eyes.
Teenagers, Rey thinks.
  Francisco is having
an art opening, Rey says,
  we should probably show up.
She gets out of bed.
  I thought he couldn't paint
because of the medicine.
  Oh he stopped taking it.

It's a series of witches and
burning oracles.
She nods okay.
Got this today in the mail,
she says handing
Rey the photograph.

From your mom?
Yup.

*

Buyers are raving!
Fox Prints! Multiple people
have given this shop a five-star
review. Commissioned a painting of
an Arctic fox and she sent two so I could
choose. Well, I couldn't. Got a bonus fox
watercolor postcard. My fox painting was
meticulously wrapped. Just the right colors,
calming and peaceful. Commissioned a pic of
a fox and received an abstract of toxic blue-
green algae. Buyers are raving! Bonus water-
color of a semiconductor chip. Trash compact-
or methodically wrapped. The smog was just
the right colors, calming and peaceful.

*

I look at the print of your
eyes in a forest of texts your cor-
respondences in the text
of forest on the floor you
are naked and I'm in Paris
full of orange seahorse-
shaped light pouring
through the balcony curtain,
you say you think of fucking me
before you give your talk
for the Royal Society
of Ornithologists in New Orleans
Rey, I'm in Tallahassee
. . . in Vermont . . . L.A.
. . . Indiana . . . . Mexico City I'm in . . .
-side: the clamor on the street,
data that's fallen away
that's turned my hair gray
from the stanzas and I'm also a thread
of poetic thought that has taken me
to a landscape past recognition,
to the chasm of dusk that wraps
around the cemetery's oval cedars
I have said too much

*

No, say more.
There are people, Paul,
who have never
been destroyed
by love, and I don't
think it's an exaggeration

that they walk among us
—the untouched—
practical as sieves.

Sometimes these people
are highly intelligent,
sometimes they
don't feel
deeply enough,
so when the opportunity
comes, they don't
even notice.
I, Cassandra, called myself
The Destroyer of Things
and prepared to wade into the metro;
Barbès-Rochechouart filled me with
punctuation and the broken
hands of ghosts.

*

Skipped school.
Seventeen years old
and had already
almost died
halfway
across the world,
so what could they
possibly teach me?
Got into UCLA
anyway. Went
to Venice Beach
to smoke weed
out of an apple
with my boyfriend

and to look at sunglasses. Queasy
lines, he was nice. Also a Jew.
The sunglasses
were hearts
and if you bought them
for me now,
my narrative
would turn to
iridescent river
weeds. Raised by
a single mom, etc.
Me too. Grew
up in the Valley, etc.
When I was wasted,
he was very sweet,
made me drink
lots of water. His mom
watched TV
all day. He would
scold her for this
but hey, that's life.
I broke up with him
for no reason.
Can't remember
his last name.
Evan something.

*

Watch out for the falling tree! says Rey
on the way to the opening.
Cassandra swerves
to the other side
of the road. Gallery entrance:
"Francisco Goya: Beauty, Reason,

& Clairvoyance, a Retrospective."
Rey cuts a piece of brie,
places it on a sesame cracker, plops
it in his mouth.
Extraordinary, he says looking
at the painting of a blob
of sea foam on a broomstick,
simply extraordinary.
Francisco wades
through the crowd.
You made it! he says.
Cassandra gazes
out the window,
blue rivers flow
down the street.
She looks into
Francisco's painting
and hears it cry
out, *Mom!*
Rey talks to Laura,
a biologist who studies orcas.
Blue rivers flow into seahorses,
hourglasses, and rocks.
Laura giggles, puts her
hand on Rey's shoulder.
I'm Nothing More than Green Lighting,
a Psychic Conduit *would look great*
in our den, Cassandra tells Francisco.
I'll sell it to you at a discount,
my friend.

*

Send word

My friend

Send stanzas

Send mountains & rivers

Send a fox print

Keep texting me

You are the only

Forget my anger

My debt

Sarcasm   Words   Too diffuse

Forget what I told you

Was all wrong

You are my   Words too

Meet me   In another city

Pour cold water   On the hurricane

Soften the fruit

I will be in Finland   Answer?

Never

I will be there

Or never

Have you   Been here?

Spent the evening With
I haven't Heard from
The man's eyes Full of Florida
Where did you Spend the night?

There was death
In those eyes Where have you
Been a long
Like mine
I deleted your
I was born a Fragment Forgive me

I was born a Seed of grass

*

in wind, airstream data, years
broken into carbon bits enclosed *Poetry*

by the haze of screens, cursors gasping
like a thunderstorm over Versailles *Strawberry Pie*

and inside the blooming flares of marjoram
flowers in terracotta pots, a phantom *Poodles*

maid glides through these hydraulic gardens,
these centuries of glare, cuts the stems, *Red Bull*

dries them in a marble room *Reese Witherspoon*

*

Thirteenth week of the Year of the Rat,
she hangs *I'm Nothing More*
than Green Lighting, a Psychic Conduit
in the den. *Mom!* she hears coming

from Z's room. Z tells her that orcas
are extremely intelligent, and when
they attack, they know to aim
for a shark's liver. She approaches
the painting, puts her forefinger
on the blob of sea foam. As she steps
inside the painting, the broomstick
world swirls to basalt, burgundy, ash.
Her body, the emerald river, mouth
becoming a sentence by Paul Celan:

But in you, from birth,
foamed the other spring
up the black
ray memory
you climbed to the day.

THE UNKNOWN WOMAN OF THE SEINE

Neolithic, she falls
asleep at the foot
of a tomb, depicted
in the Terracotta of Malta,
alluvium dream
of the future, they
believed this incubation
would reveal
the world's tributaries,
sucking phantoms
from sediment, waves,
wax flow of the death
mask made
by a Paris mortician
(1885), shaped
like a moth that flies
from the eye hole, or
into a mouth full
of sand, murky river water,
so taken by her beauty —
nothing dead could have
skin so smooth, cheeks
so round! — just the proximity
to the grave is enough to
predict the future,
this interlude, pause
in the stream of time,
eddy in our story,
where we spin into
a woman they believe
died between the ages of sixteen

and nineteen, her body placed
on twelve noir marble
slabs in the morgue,
as groups of teenage
boys peer through
the window — point
at her rotting breasts,
this public viewing
of her form, no blue
tulips for this
unknown dead —
but when Rainer Maria Rilke
passed by the shop and saw
her death mask
in 1905 and bought
it for Auguste Rodin,
whom he worked for
as a secretary — ochre
pigment was sprinkled
on the dead to usher
the body into the sun —
Rodin's hands plunged
into the auburn-tinted
water as he pulled a
ceramic elbow
out of the sink
to wash off a splash
of blood from a small
cut, we must
remember, the mask
says how sad it is to love
and be loved,
which is her expression
replicated by the violence

of fractals and images
as Maurice Blanchot
hangs the mask
in his parlor
and philosophizes
and we took tests
on these bankrupt
philosophies and failed
them or passed
but, in either case,
we lost ourselves
in terrible ideas
based on the lie
that her dreams could
be reproduced by men
with no connection
to our bodies, but
now we sleep
at the foot of a grave
and take in the centuries,
water that fills
the nightmare no
matter what shape
it takes or how many
waves lap against
limbs, we were so
happy sitting on
the riverbanks
in August half-
naked smoking clove
cigarettes, buying
cheap topaz dresses
with traveler's checks,
one with a fox print,

mood rings, and books
like *Anna Karenina*
we pretended to read
listening to Bob Dylan
drunk and dancing,
the source is
hardening
into art, no, art's
replication, not culture,
exactly, more a propulsion
of the crowd into the Musée
d'Orsay's exhibit of death
masks (2002), called
"Last Portrait,"
this girl's face
(Sex worker?
Peasant? New
to the city?
Love affair gone
wrong? A plain
suicide?) between
Mozart and
Robespierre,
she took one look
at the masks and
said, *okay, I'll be a poet*,
but back to the 19th-
century morgue
and the decaying
hands and feet of
photographer
Hippolyte Bayard,
who is the first
person to stage

a suicide in
photography: behold
the bloated corpse

fished from
the Seine! yet,
from this supposed
morgue scene
there is a nice, clean
straw hat hanging
behind him, which
gives away the hoax,
and when the self-
portrait is complete,
he walks to a nearby
café and complains
to a friend about
the annoying
attention Louis Daguerre is
getting from his pictures
of the catacombs, flux
morph, scales, the unknown
woman's death mask

landed in the hands
of Norwegian
toymaker Asmund
Laerdal, whose two-year-old son
almost drowned in 1940,
and when he pulled
the child from the river,
he decided to
create "Anne,"
the CPR doll
we all recognize today,
she is sometimes called
the "most kissed
face of all time,"
who comes back
to life, sometimes,
but dies often, like art,
you never know
what will happen,
muse drowned
in her own fluvial
dreams, ecstatic
half-smile, it was Claire
Goll who accused
Paul Celan of plagiarizing
her husband Yvan's
poetry, there
are many letters
where Paul
defends himself
against the attacks,
the entire literati
is turning

against him,
and he talks
about how humiliating
it is to have to defend
yourself against people
who want
to kill you,
and he recounts
in his letter to
Alfred Andersch
on 7/27/56 that Claire
summoned sculptress
Chana Orloff to cast a death
mask of her still-
living husband,
and Chana ran away
horrified, which is
strange because
in 1936 Claire
wrote a short story called
"The Unknown Woman
of the Seine," in which
a man dies of a heart attack
upon looking at
a death mask
believing it is his
daughter's, and most certainly
what pushed Paul Celan,
whom many regard
as a kind of 20th century seer,
giving his poems
almost prophetic agency,
to jump in the Seine

was depression and anxiety
made more acute
by Claire's false
accusations,
but it is ecstasy, not depression,
typical of ancient seers
like Cassandra, a positive
madness, bolts of language
twisted around oracles, this love
between the gods and psychics,
a language fused into itself
like an ebony box of vibration,
the prophesies moving
up the thighs, a sexual delight
in hair and the wet
body, glittering
as if having bathed
in a river, and now
she knows things
others don't through
sitting at the foot
of the grave, which
is another word for river,
all that history
on the backs of simple
people, the weight
unbearable, it isn't
fair, crowds
flowing down
the boulevards,
the market
open, an old woman
buying produce, a

week later, she, too,
would be dredged
from the river,
clutching
one onion
in each hand.

ON FRANCISCO GOYA

1. Contracted the "mysterious disease of Bordeaux" in 1793. From that point on, he became a depressive.
2. Obsessed with painting the Rhine.
3. FICO score is 510; his sister's score is 800.
4. Draws a woman holding her dying lover on the wall of his farmhouse with charcoal.
5. Drives his 1978 Oldsmobile Toronado through the verdant swamps of Tallahassee to therapy. The therapist smokes weed and wears a long dress with violets printed on it.
6. Laura, his sister, researches orcas and doesn't understand art. She says Francisco uses her. *Look*, she says, pointing to the farmhouse wall, *You've reduced my face to skin and bone!*
7. When Francisco is angry at someone (now, Laura) he uses a purple wash for their portrait, which will later become the most valuable and striking aspect of his work.
8. Laura shows Francisco how to open the door of her pearl-white Tesla.
9. Francisco has never painted a fox.
10. Has visions of pigeons, sacks, cages, saws, iron, hair clippings, pullies and levers, hoes, asylums, dogs, ladders, lanterns, tongs, rags, aprons, sandbags, hooks, helmets, flax, tin, scalpels, rods, axes, ropes, picks, wire, crab pots, screws, nets, bolts, nuns flowing through convent doors.

III)

I walk in curious, rainy
steps further and further
from Hotel Precipice: ghosts
vaporized against
coregulated wallpaper, trace the Seine
with my forefinger
on the phone's map, cut
glass nicks thumb, between two
mirrors, your face, and words that sit — *poetry*
always true — on an incline — *always*
faithful — slip
into the pyrite century.
From the wrought iron
window of Hotel Precipice,
I see a woman in riding
clothes walk her beige Afghan,
slender legs like the furred
porcelain of Oppenheim's tea-
cup, as orange light arcs
a cacophony through
the tiny bones
of my spread hand.

*

My hands: their hypnagogic
bones wrapped around
my little Walkman, sweet
sixteen, running through
a wheat field outside
Hamburg, listening to
Pink Floyd, desperate

to burn calories.
At least, aunt Caroline
says, *you turned*
your pain into poetry.
When you were
in Germany, so anorexic, I wanted
to come rescue you,
but your mother
said to leave you there.

You like . . . *Antiquarian Sticker Books.*

Plath's *ich ich ich* means nothing
to me anymore: sounds like static from 1994.
Sounds like my lineage fizzling,
frayed wire,

You like *Boho Aesthetic*

You like *Creative Writing*

Bend in the river
or wind, terrible cross
between wolves and trains.

*

Strolled
down Fairfax Ave.
one evening—
bought a pastrami
sandwich on rye bread,
vintage maroon
leather coat.
That was the start

of something. My dad
rented an apartment in
Beverly Hills for me.
Sixteen, lived alone.
He spent time away.
Doing what?
Laurel Ave.
Don't know.
Worked for
the government.
Wilshire Blvd.
Married five times.
Better not to know.
Started writing poetry.
There's my diary
right here.
I wrote: "memories thrown
together like
a strange puzzle."
I wrote: "what if I'm
the daughter of a fox?"
I wrote: "I will become
a great poet or die."
I wrote: "my heart
is a copper ruin."

La Cienega. Something
monstrous flickered
my fingertips. If this
was a Bildungsroman and not
an elegy or family history,
I would say it was the day
I really saw . . .

Or if this was a love poem
to two poets . . .

*

. . . If this was ecstasy
captured in a painting of
a goat with horns
wrapped in oak leaves
under the crescent moon . . .

*

Back in L.A.
from Germany,
my mother
kicked me out,
couldn't handle it.
I ask my aunt why
she would yell at her
for trying to help me?
She was raised
by Holocaust survivors.

[Something silent goes on this line].

I sprinkle dried parsley
on the poached eggs.

*

I called a guy. We took
the elevator
to the top
of a metallic hotel
in Santa Monica.

All that glass
and iron.
Nothing bad
happened. We talked
about Bob Dylan
or Rilke. *Paris,*
infinite show place . . .
the restless ways
of the world . . .
He asked me to
read his screenplay.
It was good.
Later he made a movie
with Kirsten Dunst.
I'm getting offtrack.
Those endless ribbons . . .
Veteran Ave.
So many white crosses.
L.A. River.
He got kicked
out of film school,
spent all his money
on a Cadillac and cocaine.

*

Francisco paints
a monk kneeling

in meditation, white
chalk, rolls of fat, face

smothered by black
tangles of Cassandra's hair.

*

She drives
through the city
endlessly, slows down
by the homeless shelter,
the one concerned
citizens say should
be removed because it's
too close to the university.
No one has seen her mother
in over two years.
Only the stereoscopes
sent with no return address,
so she drives in circles,
octagons, squares,
triangles, in rages, in sobs,
in memories, in futures,
in distances, in
this intimacy called
the leaf vein
of the present moment.
Mom will die
and you won't know.
Dusk falls and the trees
are still falling
across the city.
Look out, Cassandra!
She considers driving
under one but swerves
to the other side.
Chloe's quarters fall
from the dashboard

onto the pink sea-
horse stain
on her lap.
The coins are very shiny
and look at her like
the eyes of reptiles.
Text from her colleague
Emily: *Are you down*
to write a paper on
Paul Celan for our panel
at the Annual Conference
of Mystical Studies?

*

What if I write a poem instead?

That might work.

Or letters?

*

Dear Paul,

The obsidian sands of Reynisfjara
decanted my phone in hourglass

couplets. The car got stuck in mud; we
pushed it out, and I felt as strong as singing.

In my journal, plants scribbled: sheep's sorrel,
tea-leafed willow, crowberry, alpine

mouse ear. I must reveal something:
I am composed of fog, and my ears are chilly!

The gusts there were terrible, ripped
our car door right off, and it tumbled

through a watery wind that remembers
everything in nested polygons.

This is where I found a collection
of omens captured in one cold, volcanic stone.

*

But not just   this stone   of Iceland
      Also, the   crystalline fractal   of a teardrop
sliced in two   by oblivion   and her spear
      Think I think I   in talismanic triplets, in
Talmudic queries   of liquid   slashes
      and move   like a serpent   down this
cobblestone path   toward the train
      tracks coming   to see you, bringing
the weathered stone, but   you already know
   what the dead know   with their   mouths
      of mosaic twilight   and bone

*

In the whoosh
      of the metro, a little girl
            with purple barrettes
                              in her hair
            sitting across from me says,
                  Look, lady, there's a dog
                  in my bag.
                  Lady, do you see it?
      There's a dog in my bag!
         She opens the bag.
            I look.

There's nothing
inside except
the grave, a short
walk from here.

*

Francisco paints Cassandra atop
a corpse playing mandolin.

Blotch of sea.

Blotch of sea
with claws, nose, and hood.

Two teens with swords
locked standing on a tree's shadow.

Woman with load
on back praying to God
while white poodle prances away.

Graphite sun shining
on work boots.

Two ghosts hunched
over reading in moonlight.

Sea blotch with clutch
of Cassandra's coal hair.

Magician's hands
touching shadow
of dead body.

Donkey carrying
Cassandra's mother toward death.

*

Also in the thirteenth week
of the Year of the Rat
Rey attends the annual meeting
of the Society of Ornithologists
and Whale Researchers
in Estes Park, Colorado.
The apartment, Rey says from the plane
has flooded. Cassandra rolls
her eyes, a river divides
the city, and he's been living
on the other side. When he
lands in Colorado, he opens his phone:
Subject: New Mail from Mom . . .

From Francisco: *New painting.*
I'm calling it, I Am a Liquid Shadow.
From Laura: *heyyyyy . . . . you at the hotel?*

*

Aeschylus gave Cassandra 258
lines in *Agamemnon* and wrote
the last of them walking to a party.

Back at Hotel Precipice Cassandra scribbles
"New Life?" in her diary, copies a quote—

In horror she discovered she belonged
to the strong part of the world — Clarice Lispector

Next day, a falcon dropped a dead
tortoise on Aeschylus's head,
killing him instantly.

Oh strange death!
We've become so technical
that even a threatening email from
a boss seems "human." Today in Paris,

no text from Rey, only the sublimity
of raspberry cream mille-feuille,
just the rain-glazed streets, fumes
of lavender, salt, and exhaust.

Still, *I am affirmation, I am ecstasy*,
the wildness of a point
of departure that splits open
the fragment into gutted atoms —
and I taste, methinks, the everliving grass,

a quote Scriabin carried
to the Himalayas because he believed
language and music could conjure
the end of the world. And under

the fragment, Cassandra
discovers a poem she wrote
in the diary of her old life, composed
a few months before marriage:

Rey, the engagement ring
you gave is   a black
diamond   from outer
space, so it's clear.   I'm about

to marry you,   The Hunter.
Will we be   happy, Fox?

I've seen the crimson things
you've dragged   behind you
stare at me   in terror.

Why is it, then, that   I'm the one
with the blue   spear
in my left   hand,   the one

birthing   and bearing
a scorpion   constellation
in the shape   of my kill?

ON PAUL CELAN

1. From his biography, we know that Paul was the hypotenuse of a love triangle. The other sides were his wife, Gisèle Lestrange, and lover, Ingeborg Bachmann, though they are not characters in this book.
2. In this text, the triangle's sides are Reynard, Cassandra, and Francisco. Paul is the center point, a grave in the middle of a triangular plot of land.
3. It is certainly possible that Paul is related to Cassandra. When one looks at the family tree, when we plot the data, a sycamore grows through a map of Paris.
4. In 1854, Robert Schumann jumped into the Rhine and was rescued by fishermen.
5. When asked why he jumped, he said that he was driven mad by the never-ending sound of the note A.
6. When Paul leapt into the Seine, legend has it he heard the note *F*.
7. The *F* could stand for "Fuck You," but the legend is recorded in French, not English.
8. My kids like to ask Siri how to say *seal* in French.
9. *Fuck fuck fuck*, says Siri through her mechanized vocal cords. My children will always laugh at this.
10. Paul is buried in a suburb far from the center of Paris because he is an outskirt, like all great poets.
11. Outskirts are what define poetry.
12. The middle is a joke Reynard laughs and laughs at. The outskirt is the mellow pear picked from a tree in the orchard of the future.
13. Claude Monet also jumped into the Seine. If he had not lived, no Impressionism.
14. We have travelled a long way, you and I.
15. Letter from Paul Celan to Ingeborg Bachmann: *You must cut off all contact with me. I can take no more, Ingeborg. No more phone calls. No more letters.*
16. We have travelled together on the metro and in the streets. We have seen the past and the future, together.

17. We have collected our data in Styrofoam cups.
18. *Chocolate chip cookie dough. Rustic cabins. Lava lamps.*
19. We have collected our strophes drenched in rainwater.
20. We have all the information we need, but it is a broken, stained-glass
    window we were instructed to swallow.
21. What can I say about terrible things that splash in the dark?
22. There are many rivers in poetry, all of them full of limbs.
23. How could we possibly reach the end of poetry?
24. By walking upstream with our hands tied behind our backs.

IV)

So, I stayed,
stayed a long time.
I came to leave
the Icelandic stone.
You said, *No, I want you*
to take *a stone.* But it's someone
else's. You said rest.
I rested. You said look up.
I looked up. October sun
streaming in disaster firmaments.
You said take a nap. I wrapped myself
in the chocolate mink coat I bought
for thirty Euros in a shop full of dust,
urine, sweat. *Take a stone,*
you insisted. I took
the prettiest one.
Looked like bone.
See? That wasn't so difficult,
was it? It glittered.
It was bloody.
Now, rest, you're
getting a cold.
Then a gray cat with
the seagrass eyes
of the underworld walked
by and purred—
you better do what he says.

*

Hello Rey.
Hello Cassandra.

Why are you calling me?
Because I miss you
and I didn't mean to.
No one knows
who says which lines.
Possible that they
weren't said.
She eats
an almond croissant.
Have you made it
to Celan's grave yet?
What do you mean, Rey?
It's only been
two days.
Crumbs on her dress
where the seahorse
was bleached.
Where did you go today?
Museum.
Can you give me
the details, baby?
I don't feel like talking.
Dark apartment.
It's late in Paris.
Dogs barking
on the street.
For a writer,
you don't really
communicate well.
She suddenly
remembers
the dream she had
on the plane —
Francisco Goya painting

her portrait.
I'll call you tomorrow.
Who says this?
Don't forget to pay for Chloe's
swim lessons.
Who says this?
Rey hangs up
her portrait: sea blotch
with hood.

*

Francisco paints a bag of human limbs
slung over a man's shoulder.

Cassandra drinking
from a large, copper bowl.

Rotten leaves near
the sketch of a woman's foot.

Young woman sitting
on a bench holding a basket
ignoring man leering at her.

A witch
with half-opened mouth,
wrinkled brow, and wide-open eyes.

*

We are speeding
down the Georgia highway
at night. Laura's
orgasm in the hotel

in Estes Park,
Colorado. At the very end
of wars, tragedies
occur. The deer
was already
dead. They were
told to go
to a shelter.
I can feel
my brain
shake
in my skull.
Laura puts on
her violet bra.
My great-aunt
wanted to stay
behind "just for
ten minutes."
What the fuck
did we drive
over? Get off
at this exit.
They didn't
have time
to see
the extinguishing
fill the sky.
Bang! White
intestines
hanging
from the fender
of the Corolla.
Bang! Bang!
In bed, she tells Rey

the orca is so smart
that when it attacks a shark,
it knows to go right
for the liver.
It was coming
for them all along.
I throw up
by the gas pump.
Their names replaced
with rock: granite,
marble, obsidian.
How do we know
it was a deer?
Their bodies
replaced with
the metamorphic: chalk,
coal, flint.
I squeeze my rose
quartz necklace.
The deer's dead
body bursts
with decayed
leaves, words.

*

Mirrory magnetic
crash as storm.
Thinned limbs in
glass reflection
at a bus stop. Berlin,
1993. Memetic particles
of words as rain.
I hadn't seen myself since . . .
the day I started

to eat again. The bus stop
fractures my body
to clean cut bones
and ruined organs
watered back
to pumping cells.
Hot dogs. Nutella.
Steak. I threw up
because my body
didn't understand
my flesh anymore.
I kept on. Hamburgers.
Bread. Orange juice.
Threw up until I saw
all the colors
Goethe had painted
his summer home. God
said, *Just look*
what you've done
to yourself. Slowly,
I came back to life.
God must be. Mustard.
Granola. Sprite.
Why can't I read
this without wincing?
Cerulean Ruin. Shadow Ruin.
Burnt Umber Ruin. Plain Green Ruin
of dead rivers. God said
nothing. Slowly,
the blood rushed
into the country
that was my flesh. Map
colors are dangerous.
A shale silence,

veiny passageways.
I threw up my past
every year until I got
to seventeen clocks.
The next day,
we walked to Buchenwald.

*

In 1944,
the French
Resistance
came down
from Vercors
in the mountains
to blow up
the train tracks
in Valence
to stop
the Nazis from
carrying
ammunition to . . .
. . . . My aunt
points toward
the tracks below.
I look
at the wall, see
my grandfather
leaning against
ziggurats of
indigo graffiti,
smoking a cigarette
with his comrades,
glancing at
the cumulous

clouds. To
not have had
the luxury
to think
the world
is over.

*

On the thirtieth week of the Year of the Rat,
Cassandra attends the conference
of the Society of Mystical Studies.
Location: Fort Wayne, Indiana,
roundtable on clairvoyance.
In bed the night before, she thinks,
this coverlet is dirty, stained
with bodily fluids. She imagines this
is one of those hotels the world
will abandon, and we will see it
on the internet over-
flowing with vines and rats.
Rats, she thinks. Her mother used
to say *rats* when she would drop
something or forget to do a chore.
The word *rat* inhabits the words *narrative*,
concentration camp, and *literature*.
The word *rat* even lives inside
the word *liberation*. She opens
the conference program and stares
at the name of her poem that becomes
a streaked bathroom mirror the next day,
where she sees herself brush her hair.

Emily's Paper: "Reynard the Fox and Astral Projection: Depictions in Literature."

Cassandra's Poem: "Burning Oracle, or on Visiting Paul Celan's Grave at Thiais"

Fran's Paper: "The Melancholic: Witches, Ghosts, and Demons in Francisco Goya."

*

Francisco considers
   the difference
between melancholy
   and sadness. John Keats
suffered from melancholia,
   which is a condition
that becomes apparent
   when you're too small
and don't fit in.
   It's a self-conscious fire
that can't be put out,
   a disease of the mad,
school shooters, addicts.
   A malady of the obsessive-
compulsive, thick and
   slow as tree sap.
Melancholia is a slate
   blue color that settles
over a yellow bay when
   the sun has set, join-
ing sky and sea
   with a bolt. Sadness
is the wispy, white
clouds that form
   when a friend
has broken lunch plans.
   You decide to make

a turkey sandwich instead.
It's a strained tendon — sad,
but manageable to look out
at the bay never
considering
it will turn to slate.
Melancholia cannot
be cured, whereas sadness
needs no cure. Melancholy
is the spell cast over
paintings, its tendrils
tightening around
the vital organs.
What holds
anything together?
A mind, a painting, a poem.

*

So take your hand — Rey's
orgasm at the Quality Inn
(Estes Park, Colorado) — and touch
my name, my painting,
my poem. I gaze at my hands.
Even when I was young,
they looked like wilted
peaches. A woman
with ugly hands.
Once, in Montreal
a fortune teller took
my hand and jumped
back in fear. I saw it
dangling there,
a wounded paw,
lost appendage.

*

The next day Rey
delivers his paper,
"How Pigeons Became Rats:
The Cultural-Spatial Logic
of Problem Animals," Laura
seated in the front row,
her hair burning all
her brother's drawings,
the farmhouse walls,
bleeding candelabrum,
smudged man clad only
in a loincloth crawling on a dirt
floor, charcoal dog with mange
howling at a moonless sky.
Ovid said love is a kind
of warfare. Some die. Some win.
Some wander off. Abandoned.

*

From behind the gravestone,
Rey shoots up and cackles.
All the animals
freeze. Oh Cassandra,
it's just an old
woman who's come
to hang a pot of blue tulips
in the lenticular clouds.

*

Poem written during Emily's talk:

October, my God, October: a paranoia
of kernels and tombs, a panorama watered-

down, the rouge returning to a slapped
cheek then draining away once again as if

nothing happened. That's the body, isn't it?
Ready to refill, ready to harvest, ready to paint
the walls of its own catacombs vertigo-blue.

*

Yet from it flows
the blue language,
a lava
beyond data.
I traced each letter
of your name
with my forefinger,
turned each vowel
upside down,
inside out, shook
the gold foil from
the granite,
knocked on
the consonants,
touched the weeds
growing
through head-
stone glyphs.

*

Dear Paul,

Right as Emily said . . .
Reynard throws
off his pilgrim's garb . . .
I unlocked my cracked
phone to the news of
an ex-lover's suicide,
the one I wrote a whole
damned book about . . .
She has been transported . . .
And here we are in Orlando
. . . *by a dream* . . . forever in the fuzzy
grip of our digitized madness. Him in . . .
yellow-clad witch . . . Me, in amethyst.
All the colors of ruin
combine to form
a new realism impressed on
. . . *this chain of events* . . . the burned
tongue. Should have asked
his strained astrological
sign. (Virgo? Taurus?)
Could the flames have fallen lower . . .
post-memory . . . into the wavering
atmosphere to reveal
the well . . . *of estranged*
generations . . . or doubles
from an aghast century . . .
A *question for the audience,*
is it folklore or imagination? . . .
pressed into the present moment
like a flower inside a book . . .
I think it's a factual encounter . . .
or a hole . . . *super-*

natural . . . in the sky,
the graves they dug.

*

That neither
of my grandparents
were allowed to go
to school past the age of ten,
that the *you*, troubled, has
changed — doubled, tripled
into the treble clef
of weather, the anonymous
love letter I keep writing
to stratus clouds, that I want
to tell you that even
the simplest statement (*let me in*
/ let me out)
is poetry and your eyes
are my shadows, my shadows,
the ditches of history.

*

Paul, what about dreams,
the phantasmagoria
of these jagged scenes? She pulls
Burning Oracle from a manila folder,
scans the audience. Cross-sections
of memory on slides, infant
held by my mother, who arcs over
the body — she counts six
people including Emily and Fran,
and one graduate student she recognizes
from the conference cocktail hour

the night before — the mother's
hair sweeping down in films
more brilliant than museum reels.
The seahorse stain in her lap
is gone, exhaled to torn
territories beyond cells, tomatine,
the silt at the bottom
of the Seine. You might have picked up
a small handful this time and held it
to the sky with your hand, might
have said, *this, here, is mine.*

BURNING ORACLE, OR ON VISITING PAUL CELAN'S GRAVE AT THIAIS

Woke in Paris, the clouds
broomsticks, cages.
What can I say about terrible
things that splash in the dark?
Busy doing what? Some work.
The ones murdered in the camps.
Cassandra's shoulders, epigenetically,
infused with grandmother
walking in Nice.
Each letter I touched
became a memory, eye sockets,
jars of fireflies, mother's photographs,
psychic conduits
or hallucinations.
You've come to? Weave my insignia
inside the crypt of history
that convulses
into a stag hit
by a car, spit out

on the other side
of the Luxembourg Gardens.
I reminded her of a lineage
she hated, my little
thumping heart, a green
river holding a tray
of illusions.
Pour yourself a cup
of coffee, Rey.
She is teaching the poetry
of Rilke on Zoom.
Teenagers, Rey thinks.
Data into the chasm
of personal history past
recognition. She
was a single mom, etc.
Mom! Chloe cries out.
I will be there.
There was death
in that green river,
your death, Paul,
and mine too.
I will be there
with my forefinger on
your name.
Bloody,
slender legs,
porcelain sky.
I wanted to rescue you.
I wrote my elegy,
a copper ruin.
A metallic hotel
and poached eggs in
Santa Monica.

And tangles of Cassandra's
astral hair, her collection
of omens. I look inside. There's nothing
except the sun shining
on work boots,
more vortex hair,
ecstasy.
October sun streaming,
sea glass eyes.
Hello Rey.
Who says this?
A witch with a half-
opened mouth
goes right for the liver.
At night,
tragedies occur.
Bang!
How do we know?
Decayed leaves.
Black ruin.
I threw up my past.
To think the world is over.
Slow as tree sap,
clouds that form.
We are all problem
animals, women
with ugly hands.
What if I write
a poem instead?
Rey shoots up.
Blue tulips,
streaming spirits,
stone glyphs,
the graves they dug.

Doubled. Tripled into
my shadows, the ditches
of history. Paul, what
about dreams?
I live a bad life. Sand
at the bottom of the Seine.
A mind. A painting. A poem.
Stare at me in terror.

ACKNOWLEDGMENTS

*

Thank you to the editors of the following journals, where many of these poems first appeared (in different forms): *Poetry*, *American Poetry Review*, the *Boston Review*, *New England Review*, *Copper Nickel*, and *Mississippi Review*. Some of these poems were published by Anstruther Press in a limited edition chapbook under the title *Combustible Mood.*

ABOUT THE AUTHOR

*

SANDRA SIMONDS is the author of eight collections of poetry, most recently, *Triptychs* (Wave Books, 2022). Her awards include the University of Akron Poetry Prize for *Further Problems with Pleasure*, chosen by Carmen Giménez, and the Cleveland State University Open Poetry Prize for *Mother Was a Tragic Girl*. She has been a finalist for numerous awards, including the National Poetry Series. Her first novel, *Assia* (Noemi Press, 2023), based on the life of Assia Wevill, won the 2023 Vermont Book Award in Fiction and was shortlisted for the Dzanc Fiction Prize. Her poetry, criticism, and creative nonfiction have been published in the *New Yorker*, the *New York Times*, *Best American Poetry*, *Poetry*, *American Poetry Review*, *Chicago Review*, *Granta*, *Boston Review*, *Ploughshares*, and others.